Not all dinosaurs were fierce. Some peacefully ate plants all day long. Let's go back in time and find out what dinosaurs were *really* like…

Parasaurolophus

Dinosaurs

Deinonychus

I am Tyrannosaurus rex. Say my name *tie-RAN-oh-SAW-rus REX*.

I am fierce and I am always hungry. I have got teeth like knives. I could gobble you up in one bite!

If you think I am scary, look out – Giganotosaurus is even bigger!

Giganotosaurus

6

READING ABOUT

Dinosaurs

by Deri Robins

Aladdin/Watts
London • Sydney

Contents

© Aladdin Books Ltd 2000

Designed and produced by
Aladdin Books Ltd
28 Percy Street
London W1T 2BZ

First published in
Great Britain in 2000 by
Franklin Watts
96 Leonard Street
London EC2A 4XD

ISBN 0 7496 4851 1

A catalogue record for this book is
available from the British Library.

Printed in the U.A.E.

Editor
Jim Pipe

Literacy Consultant
Rosemary Chamberlin,
Oxford Brookes University
Westminster Institute of Education

Science Consultant
Professor Michael J. Benton
University of Bristol

Design
Flick, Book Design and Graphics

Picture Research
Brian Hunter Smart

Dinosaurs lived on Earth millions of years ago. We know how they looked because people have dug up their bones and put them together.

Dinosaurs could be as big as a house or as small as a chicken. They lived on land, often in groups. Other animals could fly or lived in the sea.

Bones

3

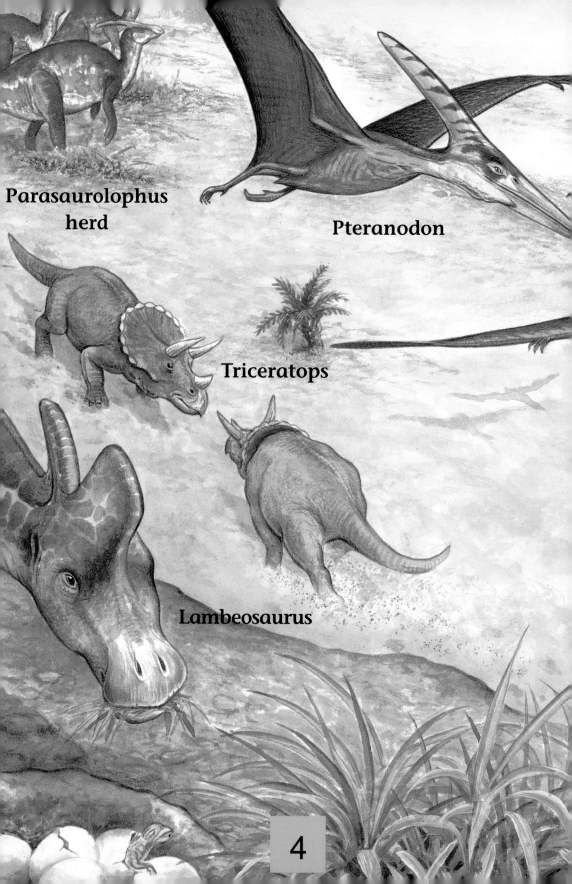

Parasaurolophus
herd

Pteranodon

Triceratops

Lambeosaurus

4

T. rex

What is it chasing?

I may look scary, but a T. rex
is also a good mother.

T. rex mother

I look after my eggs carefully.
Other dinosaurs will grab them
for a snack if I am not careful.

Once my babies hatch, I watch
over them until they are big
enough to live on their own.

Egg hatching

I am a giant Brachiosaurus.

You say my name *BRAK-ee-oh-SAW-rus*. I am as heavy as eight elephants and bigger than a bus.

Although I am so big, I will not hurt you! I eat juicy leaves, not other animals.

Brachiosaurus

Bus

Brachiosaurus spends the day munching plants with the rest of its herd. It does not mind if other plant-eaters come along. But it watches for hunters like Allosaurus.

Herds

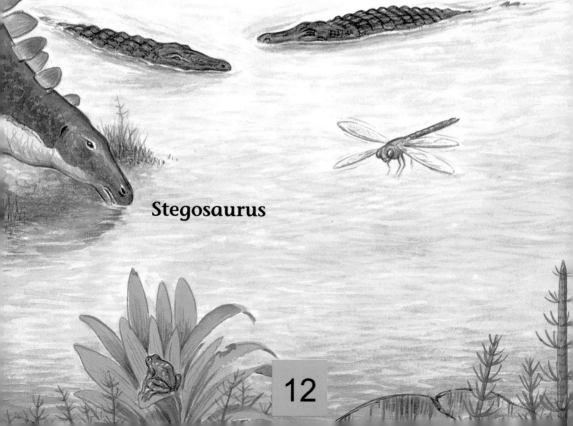

Stegosaurus

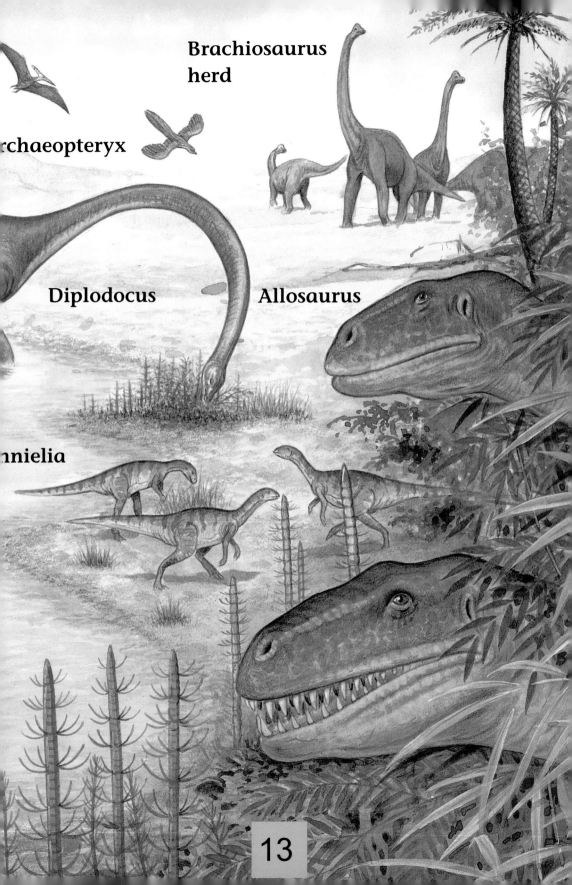

Brachiosaurus herd

rchaeopteryx

Diplodocus

Allosaurus

nnielia

13

I am Triceratops (*try-SER-a-tops*). My name means "three-horn face". I eat plants, but I charge like a rhino if anyone attacks me.

Triceratops

Ankylosaurus

Look at Ankylosaurus (say *an-KY-low-SAW-rus*)! He is like a tank on four legs. Even T. rex watches out for his swinging club tail.

I am Stegosaurus. You say my name *STEG-oh-SAW-rus*.

The plates on my back
look like armour –
but I use them to
soak up the sun
and keep
myself warm.

Stegosaurus

I am Parasaurolophus. You say my name *PAR-a-saw-ROL-o-fus*.

Parasaurolophus

The crest on my head is hollow.
I can blow it like a horn.

If I hear a T. rex crash through the
bushes, I honk my horn to warn
the herd!

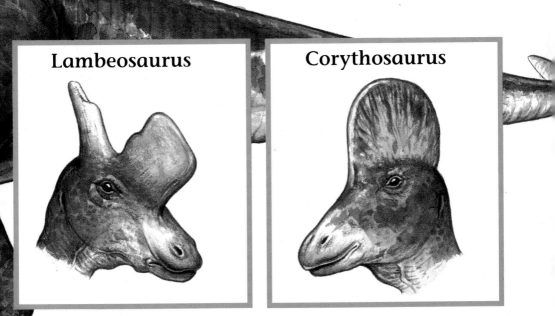

Lambeosaurus

Corythosaurus

My relatives have other crests.

19

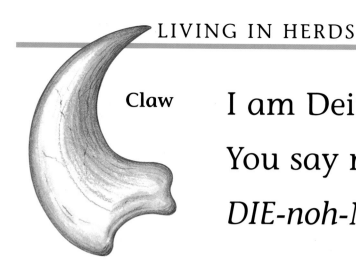

Claw

I am Deinonychus! You say my name *DIE-noh-NY-kus.*

It means terrible claw, and I have got one on each foot.

Tenontosaurus

20

I am not much taller than you,
but I am fast, fierce and deadly.

I hunt in a pack so that I can
attack bigger dinosaurs. We
quietly sneak up, then attack!

Deinonychus

Pteranodon

I am Pteranodon. You say my name *ter-AN-oh-don*. I am not a dinosaur, but a big flying reptile.

My wings are leathery, not feathery. My body is furry, just like a bat's.

Archaeopteryx (*AR-kee-OP-ter-iks*) was the first bird. People think that some dinosaurs grew feathers and took off for the skies!

Archaeopteryx

23

I am Elasmosaurus. Say my name *ee-LAZ-moh-SAW-rus*.

I am a sea reptile. I have four strong flippers to help me swim. My long neck darts out to catch fish as I swim.

Elasmosaurus

Ichthyosaurus
(*IK-thee-oh-SAW-rus*)
is a fast swimmer. It
breathes air on the
surface of the water,
like a dolphin.

Ichthyosaurus

Why did the dinosaurs die out? Nobody knows for sure.

Some people think most of them died after a giant rock crashed into the Earth from outer space.

End of the dinosaurs

Can You Find?

Dinosaurs have lots of strange parts to their body. Can you find which dinosaurs these parts come from?

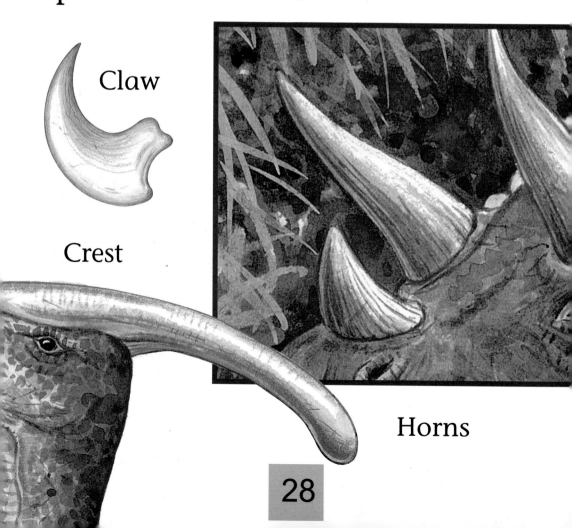

Claw

Crest

Horns

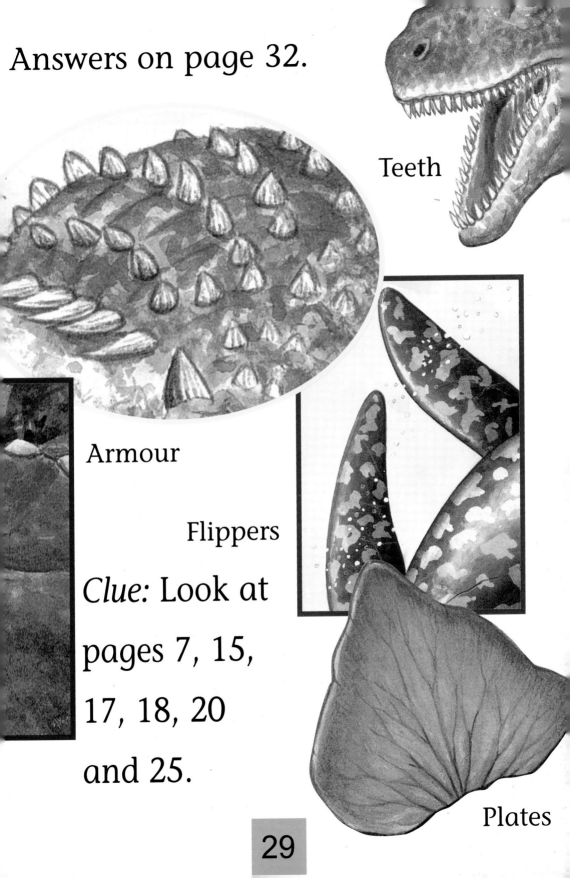

Answers on page 32.

Teeth

Armour

Flippers

Plates

Clue: Look at pages 7, 15, 17, 18, 20 and 25.

Do You Know?

Some of today's animals lived at the time of the dinosaurs. Do you know which ones they are?

Shark

Insect

The answers are on page 32.

Bird

Humans

Fish

Crocodile

Turtle

Index

ANSWERS TO QUESTIONS

Pages 28-29 – Deinonychus has this **claw** • Parasaurolophus has this **crest** • Triceratops has these **horns** • T. rex has these **teeth** • Ankylosaurus has this **armour** • Elasmosaurus has these **flippers** • Stegosaurus has these **plates**.

Pages 30-31 – **Sharks, insects, fish, turtles, crocodiles** and **birds** all lived at the time of the dinosaurs, but **humans** did not. Did you see the crocodiles and insect on page 12, and the birds on pages 4-5?

Photocredits: Abbreviations: t-top, b-bottom, r-right, l-left, c-centre.
3, 31c – The Natural History Museum, London. 11br – Scania. 30c, 31tl, 31tr, 31bl, 31br – Digital Stock. 30br – Stockbyte.
Illustrators: Alan Baker; Wayne Ford – Wildlife Art Ltd.